The Art of War

Also by Yvette Nolan

Annie Mae's Movement
Medicine Shows: Indigenous Performance Culture
Performing Indigeneity (edited with Ric Knowles)
Reasonable Doubt (with Joel Bernbaum and Lancelot Knight)
Refractions: Scenes (edited with Donna-Michelle St. Bernard)
Refractions: Solo (edited with Donna-Michelle St. Bernard)
The Unplugging

The Art of War

Yvette Nolan

Playwrights Canada Press
Toronto

The Art of War © 2025 by Yvette Nolan
First edition: August 2025
Printed and bound in Canada by Imprimerie Gauvin Ltée, Gatineau

Jacket art by Alfred Bastien, *Canadian Gunners in the Mud, Passchendaele*, CWM 19710261-0093, Beaverbrook Collection of War Art, Canadian War Museum
Author photo by Nadya Kwandibens

Playwrights Canada Press
202-269 Richmond St. W., Toronto, ON M5V 1X1
416.703.0013 | info@playwrightscanada.com | www.playwrightscanada.com

LIBRARY AND ARCHIVES CANADA CATALOGUING IN PUBLICATION
Title: The art of war / Yvette Nolan.
Names: Nolan, Yvette, author.
Identifiers: Canadiana (print) 20250174707 | Canadiana (ebook) 20250178036
| ISBN 9780369105585 (softcover) | ISBN 9780369105592 (PDF)
| ISBN 9780369105608 (EPUB)
Subjects: LCGFT: Historical drama. | LCGFT: Drama.
Classification: LCC PS8577.O426 A89 2025 | DDC C812/.54—dc23

Playwrights Canada Press staff work across Turtle Island, on Treaty 13 and Treaty 20 territories, as well as unceded lands, which are the current, ancestral, and future homes of the Anishinaabe Nations (Ojibwe / Chippewa, Odawa, Potawatomi, Algonquin, Saulteaux, Nipissing, and Mississauga / Michi Saagiig), the Wendat, members of the Haudenosaunee Confederacy (Mohawk, Oneida, Onondaga, Cayuga, Seneca, and Tuscarora), and the xʷməθkʷəy̓əm (Musqueam), Sḵwx̱wú7mesh (Squamish), and səlilwətaɬ (Tsleil-Waututh) Nations, as well as Metis and Inuit peoples. It always was and always will be Indigenous land.

We acknowledge the financial support of the Canada Council for the Arts, the Ontario Arts Council (OAC), Ontario Creates, the Government of Ontario, and the Government of Canada for our publishing activities.

Canada Council for the Arts | Conseil des arts du Canada
Ontario Arts Council | Conseil des arts de l'Ontario
an Ontario government agency | un organisme du gouvernement de l'Ontario
Ontario Creates | Ontario Créatif
Canada
Ontario

For all those who make art in the face of great conflict.

Foreword

Many Canadians don't know this—I didn't know it either before reading this play—but Canada's best-known visual records of war stem from four official war art programs: the Canadian War Memorials Fund from the First World War, the Canadian War Records from the Second World War, the Canadian Armed Forces Artists Program from the Cold War era, and the Canadian Forces Artists Program (CFAP), which is still running today.

The first initiative was led by Lord Beaverbrook and was privately funded. Beaverbrook envisioned war art not only as a historical record but as an expression of national identity. In the Second World War it was the artists themselves who advocated for the government to fund a similar program, which arrived three years later as the Canadian War Records.

Interest in war art was renewed during the Cold War. In 2001 the Department of National Defence launched the CFAP, which embraced all art forms: visual, literary, and dramatic. The program grants artists considerable freedom, including space for dissonance and protest. Historically these programs were largely anglophone, with limited participation from Québécois, IBPOC, and women artists—but that is changing.

When Yvette spoke to me about visiting the exhibition of Canadian wartime art housed at the Museum of Civilization (now called the Canadian Museum of History) in Ottawa, she kept returning to the image of a war artist walking alongside fellow infantry in a war zone, not carrying weapons but sketchbooks and paintbrushes. Artists risking their lives to witness, to feel, and to translate that chaos into something the people back home might begin to understand.

This image would not leave her, and it's what compelled her to write *The Art of War*.

Our protagonist, Nick, wears a soldier's uniform, but he doesn't pick up a gun. He is a war artist, tasked with capturing a truth too large, too fragmented, and too painful to hold. His journey is one of becoming: as an artist, as a witness, as a human trying to find order in the chaos of war. The play poses difficult and necessary questions about the cost of being an artist. What does it take to tell the truth? What does it mean to be an artist when the world is burning and art feels both vital and insufficient?

Reading this play reminds me of what art offers in times of war, pandemic, or personal upheaval, when we are searching for clarity in the chaos. Artists walk the front lines of grief, transformation, and resilience. It's no small task. We face fear, burnout, poverty, and self-doubt. We question our purpose, our impact, our voice. And still, artists show up. Because art is how we make sense of what we value as human beings.

This story comes at a time when war once again dominates the headlines. Iran, Gaza, Ukraine, Sudan. We are not immune, nor are we separate. The questions at the heart of this play are not historical—they are immediate.

Yvette, so beautifully through the character of Nick, is insisting we must persist. Despite the noise, the fear, the uncertainty, we must keep going, we must try to make sense of the senseless for ourselves, for our communities, for the future.

It's a kind of hope we need, which is why this play makes me cry every time I read it.

All My Relations,
Keith Barker

Keith Barker is a Métis artist from Northwestern Ontario and Director of the Foerster Bernstein New Play Development Program at the Stratford Festival. The former artistic director of Native Earth Performing Arts, Keith has received the Johanna Metcalf Prize, the Dora Mavor Moore Award for Outstanding New Play, and the Playwrights Guild of Canada's Carol Bolt Award for his playwriting. He is the director of The Art of War *for the 2025 Stratford Festival season.*

The Art of War was first produced by Hardly Art Theatre at the Remai Arts Centre BackStage Stage, Saskatoon, on November 9–12, 2023, with the following cast and creative team:

Newman: Joshua Beaudry
Dennis and Matthaeus: Skye Brandon
Heather, Magda, and Eva: Amanda Trapp
Nick: Colin Wolf

Director: Yvette Nolan
Set and Prop Designer: Taegan O'Bertos
Lighting Designer: Michelle Ramsay
Costume Designer: Jensine Emeline
Sound Designer: Grahame Kent
Props Coordinator: Rory Jewiss
Lighting Associate: Judith Schulz
Stage Managemer: Johanna Arnott
Original Art: Iris Hauser
Dramaturg: DD Kugler

The play was later produced by the Stratford Festival from August 1 to September 27, 2025, with the following cast and creative team:

Nick: Josue Laboucane
Newman: Jordin Hall
Magda: Jenna-Lee Hyde
Heather and Eva: Julie Lumsden
Dennis and Matthaeus: Rylan Wilkie

Director: Keith Barker
Set Designer: Teresa Przybylski
Costume Designer: Patricia Reilly
Lighting Designer: Logan Raju Cracknell
Sound Designer: Adam Campbell
Stage Manager: Kelly Luft
Assistant Stage Manager: Suzanne McArthur
Apprentice Stage Manager: Ava Robitaille

Characters

Nick
Newman
Magda
Heather
Eva
Dennis
Matthaeus

Blank Canvas

In the darkness we hear HEATHER *delivering a lecture in 2005. As the lights come up, the sounds of war begin to overcome her voice.* NICK *is standing at attention centre stage, nearly naked. As the sounds of war increase,* NICK *dresses in a soldier's uniform.*

HEATHER: . . . it can be argued that the war made Canadian art and Canadian artists, who in turn made Canada. A. Y. Jackson, Arthur Lismer, and Frederick Varley, all original members of the Group of Seven, were war artists during the First World War, Lawren Harris during the Second World War.

Alex Colville, who has been referred to as the "painter laureate" of Canada, was also a war artist during the Second World War, as was Charles Comfort, who went on to run the National Gallery . . .

As the chaos reaches a crescendo, NICK *finishes dressing and reaches for his weapon, his brushes and pencils, canvas, and sketchbook. He presents arms. Everything stops. And fades.*

Newman 1

NICK painting. NEWMAN arrives.

NEWMAN: Shouldn't you be somewhere painting naked women and seducing officers' wives?

NICK: Newman!

The two men embrace.

NEWMAN: I heard you'd been plucked to be a war artist. One minute you were there, crawling beside me with the sergeant hollering at us to keep our rifles outta the dirt, and then you were gone.

NICK: Not exactly plucked. We had to fight for it. Seems everyone had forgotten we'd already sent artists to war. Jackson was wounded as a soldier then went back in as an artist. Varley was an artist and a soldier during the Hundred Days that ended the war—

NEWMAN: yeah well that was the war to end all wars, wasn't it? they forgot that part too

NICK: I wanted to paint, Newman, wanted it so badly. I went after the commission, begged to be allowed to be an artist, and not just a soldier—

NEWMAN: *just* a soldier?

NICK: I didn't mean—

NEWMAN: I know what you mean, Nick. One artist per division. The other fifteen thousand of us are expendable.

NICK: it's just—some of us were already trained as artists, seems a waste to not use us

NEWMAN: a real waste

NICK: it's important that we're here—

NEWMAN looks at NICK's canvas.

NEWMAN: It's . . . nice, Nick. But you coulda painted this back in Nova Scotia.

NICK: I know. Except I didn't. The day job, Fran . . . and I got rusty. This is practise. Practising the relationships, trees to sky, light through leaves. Perspective. Slow stuff. It's like recovering a language you learned as a child. The hand has to remember how it's connected to the eye, and to the heart. I'm grateful for the opportunity to practise the craft.

NEWMAN: Not as good as a naked woman, but it's nice. Peaceful.

NICK: Peaceful. Huh.

NEWMAN: Yeah. That's funny, right? Send an artist to war to paint peaceful pictures—what's that word—that word for this kind of scene? with lambs grazing and shepherds and stuff

NICK: pastoral

NEWMAN: pastoral! exactly!

NICK: You're right. That is funny.

NEWMAN picks up NICK's sketchbook and flips through.

NEWMAN: It's not exactly a bowl of fruit and a dead pheasant, is it?

NICK takes it back.

NICK: No, it's a ton of potatoes and a side of beef.

NEWMAN: Still still life, I guess.

NICK: yeah. I wish I could get out there but I'm nowhere near the front—

NEWMAN: Be careful what you wish for, pal.

NICK: Everyone thinks this'll be over quick now that the Yanks are in.

NEWMAN: Not quick enough for me.

NICK: So you've seen action, Newman

NEWMAN: I've seen things I'll never forget till the day I die, Nick. And I volunteered. Christ.

NICK: too bad you're not the artist then

NEWMAN: Paint me.

NICK: Newman

NEWMAN: yeah, yeah, c'mon. I'm a soldier, I've seen action, I'll do a re-enactment

NEWMAN grabs his gun and poses.

attention! no, no, wait, action shot!

NEWMAN crouches as if advancing under fire.

NICK laughs.

come on!

NICK: how long do you think you'll be able to hold that pose?

NEWMAN: how long do you think you'll have to make a sketch in the field? Now *this* is practise.

NICK: okay, hold on

NICK flips to a blank page in his sketchbook, grabs a pencil, starts to sketch NEWMAN.

NEWMAN: Isaac was always scritching away in his little book. Pinned down by mortars, he's scribbling away. after lights out he's burning his fingers on match after match, scritch scritch scritching away—

NICK: who's Isaac?

NEWMAN: you remember Isaac

NICK: was he in basic with us?

NEWMAN reaches in his pocket and pulls out a small journal.

NEWMAN: Yeah. No. I don't know. Doesn't matter. Maybe he was before your time. Isaac's always scribbling away in his journal. And for what? Bloody poetry. Listen, listen to this:

"In his malodorous brain what slugs and mire,
Lanthorned in his oblique eyes, guttering burned!"*

* Isaac Rosenberg, "God," (~1916 or before). Rosenberg died at the front in 1918.

Cripes.

NICK: Where'd you get that?

NEWMAN: Told you. Got it offa Isaac.

NICK: Don't you think you'd better give it back?

NEWMAN: He's not going to need it where he's gone, my friend.

NICK: Oh.

NEWMAN: "Who rests in God's mean flattery now? Your wealth
Is but his cunning to make death more hard."

I don't get it. I should chuck the thing away, or send it to his folks. But for now I carry it around, open it up once in a while, and try to figure out what the hell he's talking about.

NICK: I didn't think you were the poetry type, Newman

NEWMAN: I'm not! But the way he talks about it, I almost get it. Like he's talking about his own—you know—

NICK nods, still sketching.

you're gonna need a smaller book

NEWMAN holds up Isaac's journal.

if you're gonna do this under fire. Or maybe you could make little cards, tuck 'em in your pockets, or up your sleeves, so you could just pull one out, make a quick sketch, slip it back. Be good to have something to put it in to protect it. See, some of these pages in Isaac's book, stuck together, mud, or blood, can't even read 'em—

NICK: Okay, that's good, Newman.

NEWMAN straightens up.

NEWMAN: can I see?

He looks at the sketch.

not bad, Nickie, not bad.

NICK: well, it gives me something to work from. They want "action episodes" from "eyewitness records" or "reconstruction." If I ever see some action, I'll insert you and it'll be both eyewitness and reconstruction.

NEWMAN: I look kinda scared

NICK: you're under fire

NEWMAN: lemme give you something else. Something heroic. Make me look like a hero. Immortalize me—

There is a single shot. NEWMAN falls. NICK hits the ground, grabs at NEWMAN.

NICK: Newman?

NEWMAN dies. NICK lies there, holding his hand, keeping his head down.

Magda 1

MAGDA enters dressed as a peasant woman. She looks around, sees no one but NICK, who is painting. She approaches him.

MAGDA: Please. Food.

NICK: Oh—

MAGDA: Food?

NICK: I—don't have anything. Um.

He pats himself, pulls things out of pockets—nothing—then:

I have a bar of chocolate. You can have it.

MAGDA takes it.

MAGDA: Chocolate.

She devours it.

NICK: sorry it isn't more.

MAGDA: Thank you.

NICK: Listen, if you come into camp, I'm sure we can—

MAGDA is alarmed, scuttling away.

MAGDA: No, no, no—

NICK: Okay, okay. It's all right. It's just—I don't have anything else to give you.

She nods, sits, exhausted.

I'm sorry.

MAGDA: It has been a long time since I tasted chocolate.

NICK: Do you live around here?

MAGDA: Today I live around here.

NICK: Because if you were going to be here tomorrow, I would bring—

MAGDA: Someone to arrest me?

NICK: Food. Something more than chocolate.

MAGDA: I don't think I will be here tomorrow.

NICK: I wouldn't—you don't have to be afraid of me.

MAGDA: I am not afraid of you. But I only trust me. Perhaps you mention to someone, I met this woman in the forest. And that person is curious, or helpful. Perhaps he means well. And he takes me and puts me in a camp, as a refugee. And perhaps the keepers of the camp are good people. For now. But this war. There is no food, most of it goes to the soldiers. And who is to say who will control the camp in a week? In two? Today the Allies are here, but that's today. I prefer to take my chances with the cows.

NICK: I'll probably be here again this week if weather holds. If you were still in the neighbourhood.

MAGDA: You come to paint?

NICK: I come to paint.

MAGDA: A soldier who paints.

NICK: Yes.

MAGDA: Or a painter who soldiers.

NICK: Not much of either right now, I'm afraid.

MAGDA: You're not American.

NICK: Canadian.

MAGDA: A Canadian painter-soldier.

NICK: I know. Fiddling while Rome burns.

MAGDA: Don't feel sorry. I think it's very civilized of Canada to send painters to war. It shows . . . imagination.

NICK: This war will become a part of the national psyche, and we'll need a way to talk about it.

MAGDA: It must be some kind of Canadian genius to think of this. "I know what we're doing over there, but what are we really doing over there?"

NICK has grabbed his sketchbook.

NICK: Is it all right if I—?

MAGDA hesitates.

MAGDA: Turn the page.

NICK does.

Again. Three more.

NICK turns three more pages. MAGDA nods.

Now I am out of order. Now it is harder to tell what day you met the woman who ate your chocolate.

NICK begins to sketch on the page to which he has turned.

This is a funny life, painter.

NICK: I don't know if funny is the word I would use.

MAGDA: no, perhaps there is a better word in English, but I do not know it. Here we are, sitting, waiting for—what? more soldiers, someone to decide whose land this is, who gets to live here. And while we wait, you draw me into your book.

NICK: It's nice to sketch life for a change. A woman.

MAGDA: and if I do not survive this war, then I will survive in this book of a Canadian painter-soldier.

NICK nods and continues to sketch.

The Nazis are gathering up art as quickly as they can and scurrying away with it, hoarding it. They outlaw the music of Mendelssohn and Mahler, exalt the music of Wagner. He is not a bad composer, a bit bombastic. But Mendelssohn is a masterful composer as well. They understand the power of art. They understand that's where the human voice lies.

NICK: But they're not making art.

MAGDA: They are mad on destruction. Filming themselves marching like puppets, with their heads all going this way and their arms all going that way. The cameras rolling—tick tick tick—the sound of rats scurrying. They are filming in their camps, too. Filming whatever horrors they can imagine in there. Filming deaths, filming pogroms, making their pornography.

NICK: I have heard . . . rumours . . . about their camps.

MAGDA: The rumours are only the beginning of the truth. I think the world will shatter when people realize what has gone on in there

NICK has stopped sketching.

may I see?

NICK: it's just a sketch

NICK hands her the sketchbook.

MAGDA touches her own face.

MAGDA: . . .

NICK: I am not very good at—

MAGDA: don't be sorry, painter. It is a gift to be able to see myself the way another human being sees me. I just did not realize that I had become . . .

NICK: become?

MAGDA: I suppose we must all accept new ideas of ourselves. I learn to think of myself as Magda the refugee, Magda the peasant, Magda the gypsy. But I remember fine things and their purpose.

Last night I slept in a church. The beautiful things that could be taken are long gone, of course, the candlesticks and the chalice, the tabernacle and the statues. But they couldn't take the stones, the columns, and the arched ceilings, and they have not yet destroyed all the stained glass. There is no god in that building, he's gone from there. What is left is the work of man. And because god has left us, the work reflects only the human spirit, attempting to speak of something larger than itself.

Newman 2

NICK is painting. NEWMAN enters. His uniform is slightly different from the last time we saw him, a different division, different era, something.

NEWMAN: Hey, Nicholas.

NICK is stunned.

Nick? You okay?

NICK: Newman?

NEWMAN: Nick, what's wrong? You look awful.

NEWMAN grabs him by the arms, shakes him a bit. NICK feels the solidity of NEWMAN's body, then embraces him.

NICK: Newman!

NEWMAN: whoa, Nickie. Easy does it, buddy. You okay?

NICK: I saw—

NEWMAN: saw some action, did you?

NICK: you

NEWMAN: yeah, it's hard, I know, especially the first time.

NICK: Shot.

NEWMAN: you're shook up. It'll be okay.

NICK: Newman, I was there.

NEWMAN: Bad, was it? dumb thing to say, it's always bad. Gruesome.

NICK: you were—

NEWMAN: you gotta hang on to yourself, Nickie, or you'll end up flipping out every time someone drops a pan or breaks a glass. That healed me faster than anything, just wanting to get away from those loonies.

NICK: How—how long were you in the hospital?

NEWMAN: Too fucking long, I'll tell you. You get to feeling really useless, sitting there day after day, knowing your buddies are out there without you. Pretty soon, you're bugging the nurses, grabbing the doc every time he goes by. I'm barely bleeding anymore, please let me go back to the front. Man, it's a crazy world.

NICK: Yes.

> *NEWMAN picks up the painting. It is of NICK and NEWMAN, spread-eagled in the dirt, holding hands.*

NEWMAN: hey, that's clever

NICK: what?

NEWMAN: they look like—kinda like a swastika—but also kinda like they are falling through the air—even though they are on the ground—pretty good, Nick—how'd you think of that?

NICK: This is the Reconstruction school of war art. Take your eyewitness account, marry it to some other landscape you have seen along the way—

NEWMAN: and voila! it's art!

NICK: is it?

NEWMAN: of course it is

NICK: but it's constructed—what am I doing here? am I documenting? Am I just banking horror images to reconstruct after the war or after my legs are blown off and I have nothing but time

NEWMAN: Nick. Nick. Easy.

NICK: someone said to me it was smart to send artists to war because we would be able to tell people what's really going on over here

NEWMAN: I don't get why you're getting all bent outta shape. It IS your job. what's the problem?

NICK: I am making stuff up

NEWMAN: Jesus, Nick, whaddya want? You want to be one of those lousy photographers—running in and snapping—snap snap snap—there's this arrogant bastard, Dennis something, a real windbag, keeps turning up, thinks he's telling the truth because it's a photograph

NICK: photography is important, Newman. Those guys can capture things I cannot.

NEWMAN: but is it art?

NICK holds up his sketchbook.

NICK: is this?

NEWMAN grabs NICK's sketchbook, flips through it.

NEWMAN: this—this—this—god, that's gross—you have seen action

NICK goes to take the sketchbook away from NEWMAN, but NEWMAN pulls away.

Hey! This is me, isn't it? Look at that. When'd you do that, Nick? We were never in a firefight together—

NICK: You—you posed for me.

NEWMAN: when?

NICK: In a peaceful field. Remember? Pastoral?

NEWMAN: I have no recollection.

NICK just looks at him.

See? That's better than a photograph. That's true-er. Without even being in a battle, you captured the feeling of it

NICK takes the sketchbook back from NEWMAN.

NICK: I don't know . . . how to make this . . . into something that people are going to want to see.

NEWMAN: isn't it your job just to make it?

NICK: at the end of this, there will be thousands and thousands of works—maybe tens of thousands—

NEWMAN: —that's a good thing—

NICK: they'll probably just stack 'em away in a warehouse somewhere, let 'em rot.

NEWMAN: Boy, are all artists as negative as you?

NICK: Oh I think so.

NEWMAN: Now if I was a manufacturer of something—fergits—say

NICK: What's a fergit?

NEWMAN: It's just a thing, a fergit, like a widget, something you make. And not everyone can make a fergit. You have to be trained to make 'em, you have to want to make 'em, and then, even then, you might not be very good at making them. And nobody really wants them, or knows what to do with 'em, but all you need is a chance to show the world that fergits are absolutely necessary to life.

So you make fergits, and the war comes along and the guys at the top for some reason decide that they need fergits for this war. You should be overjoyed! Your big break. When this war is over, everyone will know the value of fergits, there will be a fergit in every house, dozens of them.

But here you are moaning, they'll probably just stash them in the broom closet, in the basement with the pickled beets. Well?

NICK: What do you mean I'm not very good at making them?

NEWMAN laughs.

NEWMAN: Oh my god. That was the fergit-maker. Me. I'm not very good at making fergits. You make art. You're good at it. Look. See?

NEWMAN grabs the sketchbook.

NICK grabs it back.

Jesus, I thought that all you wanted was to be paid to paint.

NICK: I am grateful for the wage and I'm grateful for the opportunity to paint.

NEWMAN: What then?

NICK: sketching it or painting it, just rendering it on paper does not make it art.

NEWMAN: How do you know? I know what I like—I like this, I don't like that.

NEWMAN takes the painting again.

I like this. It speaks to me.

NICK: I imagine it would.

NEWMAN: Because there's something of you in it.

NICK: of me?

NEWMAN: yeah. You are saying something to me here.

NICK ponders this.

That doesn't mean I know if it's good or not.

NICK: Like Isaac's poetry.

NEWMAN: Isaac's poetry?

NICK: Isaac's journal, his poetry, when you were—

NEWMAN: who the hell is Isaac?

Silence.

Nick? You're okay, aren't you?

NICK: I don't know.

NEWMAN: You have to take care of yourself, buddy.

NICK: It's like—nothing changes. When Jackson was sent to the front as an artist in the first war, he said "same old war . . . same old soldiers sticking it out . . . same old mud and shell holes."* And here I am.

NEWMAN: this is war, Nickie. Madness. You want sense out of this, you make it. YOU make it.

NICK: I don't know that I can make sense of this, Newman.

NEWMAN: not now, Nick. Later. That windbag photographer's stuck with the moment he's captured on film. Ain't never gonna be more than that. But you have time and distance. Memory. You have a chance to remember these young fellas who've been chopped down and cut up, remember them for the folks back home. For me.

NICK: For you?

NEWMAN: The war's impossible to explain in words. I try, I try to write these things to my mother, to Rosie. But there's no way to make them understand. It's horrible, I say. What do they know of horrible? There's mud. So yeah, there's mud, big deal, I'm from Saskatchewan, there's earth, occasionally there's rain, there's mud. I tell them I've seen people die, they understand dead. Dead for them means not coming back. Dead for me is always here *(taps his head)*. Dead is active, losing blood, losing breath, losing that light in the eyes. It's not just an absence. It's also a presence.

---

* A. Y. Jackson, 1917, upon his return to the front as a war artist.

NICK: That's an awful lot to expect of an artist.

NEWMAN: Of course it is.

NICK: And you're right, most of us fergit-makers are not very good.

NEWMAN: At least you've got the chance to try.

NICK: And you think people back home want to see the mud and the blood and the horror?

NEWMAN: Yes, oh yes, I do. I will want to see those things, I will want to know that what happened to me here really happened, wasn't a dream. And maybe I will be able to take Rosie to your painting, your painting of two men spread-eagled in the mud, one shot and bleeding, the other holding him to this life with just that hand, just that grip keeping him earthbound, human. And I will stand there with my arm around her waist and say, "There, it was like that, it felt like that." And she will turn and look at me and her eyes will fill up and she will hold me and help me and heal me.

NICK: I don't think I can live up to that, Newman.

NEWMAN: It's your job.

There is a shot. NEWMAN *falls into* NICK*'s arms.*

NICK: No no no no

NEWMAN: Yes

NEWMAN *dies.*

Nick Under Fire

The war is suddenly all around. A soldier runs on, advancing. He motions to NICK *to move with him, but before the soldier gets two steps along, he is hit. He falls, perhaps in slow motion, perhaps suspended. Perhaps he gets up again, dies again. Perhaps* NEWMAN *rises and dies again. It's a ballet of casualties.*

Finally, NICK *unfreezes. He reaches into his pocket, pack, whatever, and gets his sketchbook, cards, whatever, and a pencil and he begins to sketch.*

The Entertainer

NICK is painting. EVA slips in and closes the door behind her.

EVA: Hey, soldier.

NICK: Hello.

EVA: I just needed a breather from the craziness out there.

NICK: Sure.

EVA: don't get me wrong, I'm thrilled to be able to come over here and do shows for our boys, but sometimes I feel like a canary in a room full of cats. Really *hungry* cats.

NICK: We don't see a lot of women.

EVA: It shows. So how come you're hiding in here?

NICK: Just cleaning up.

EVA: Wow. And cleaning up is more interesting than trying to get a look at the showgirl?

NICK: It's not that, it's just—

EVA: I know I'm no Marlene Dietrich, but—

NICK: I can't leave my brushes out, they—

EVA: Oh, you're a painter.

NICK nods.

Can I see?

NICK: I'd rather not—

EVA: Aw, don't be shy.

She comes over and tries to look at some of his paintings. NICK is collecting things together, trying to keep things from her. He covers the painting on the easel in some way, flipping it, or putting something in front of it. She spots the sketchbook, reaches for it. She is too close. Uncomfortable, he snatches the sketchbook and pulls away. She exposes the painting.

Uh-huh.

She flips through other canvases. NICK continues to clean up.

So, why do you do this?

NICK: It's my job.

EVA: It's your job to paint Jeeps and guys loading boxes onto trucks?

NICK: It's my job to paint scenes of war. There's a lot of Jeeps and guys loading boxes onto trucks.

EVA: Seems like a weird job to me.

NICK: Me too.

EVA: So you're like an artist.

NICK: Yes, I'm like an artist.

EVA: I'm like an artist too.

NICK: Yes.

EVA: But I think it's important to entertain.

NICK: Uh-huh.

EVA: Do you have a cigarette?

NICK: Sorry, I don't smoke.

EVA: just as well. bad for my throat. Not that it matters in this kind of show. I belt out a few, and the guys are yelling and whistling too much to be listening anyway.

NICK: Oh, I'm sure they're listening.

EVA: Sometimes I wanna sing something slow and melancholy—

(sings) "What'll I do
When you are far away
And I am blue
What'll I do?"*

And all they really want is"

"The boogie woogie bugle boy of Company B!"†

---

* "What'll I Do," Irving Berlin, 1923.

† "Boogie Woogie Bugle Boy," Hughie Prince and Don Raye, 1941.

NICK: You've got a lovely voice.

EVA: Thanks. Anyway, a girl's gotta make a living. I think it's important to offer something that'll take their mind off the fighting. Take the boys' minds off death and all.

NICK: It's nice.

EVA: Nice?

NICK: It—you—remind us of home.

EVA: That *is* nice. Although if this is what you guys do most of the time

She motions to his work.

fix Jeeps and load stuff onto trucks—

NICK: We also peel potatoes and clean our guns.

EVA: Thrilling. Well, maybe offering a break from boredom is good.

NICK: there's lots of blood and guts

EVA: Do you paint that stuff too?

NICK pushes the sketchbook at her. She flips through it.

Eeuuw. Is that—?

NICK nods.

Oh my god. Now what's the point of painting something like that?

NICK: It's the truth.

EVA: Truth shmuth. It's gross. A boot with a foot in it. What kind of art is that?

NICK: It's a still life.

EVA: It's not still life, it's death.

NICK: That was a joke.

EVA: a joke is funny.

NICK: Sorry.

EVA: Look, I don't mean to offend you, but—shouldn't art be beautiful or something?

NICK: I don't know if it needs to be beautiful. But it needs to make you feel something.

EVA: This makes me feel gross. And your other stuff makes me feel bored, so is that feeling something?

NICK: Depends. Is it active boredom or just anaesthetized?

EVA: Numb. Smarty pants. See, I knew what it meant.

NICK: It wasn't a trick question.

EVA: It's not your fault. Your subject matter is not exactly beautiful. And if you were to make it beautiful—"Oh, honey, look, isn't that the most beautiful foot in a boot you've ever seen? Let's buy it and hang it in the living room just over the mantel, right next to the photographs of the grandkids"—then it would sorta defeat the purpose, wouldn't it?

NICK: That's exactly what I don't want to do.

EVA: I don't know if you could make it pretty anyway.

NICK: Lots of painters glorify war. Go into any museum here and you'll see all kinds of heroic glowing paintings of war, the soldiers look like angels and knights and saints. Glory to God, glory to war.

EVA: Maybe that's a way to keep the young men all revved up. Keep them enlisting. Keep war alive.

NICK just looks at her.

what? A girl can't have a brain and a pretty face?

NICK: I wasn't

EVA: I think you were

EVA flips through the sketchbook.

Well, you're sure not glorifying it, anyway. Were there any artists who didn't?

NICK: Glorify war?

EVA: Yeah.

NICK: Goya.

EVA: Goya? That's a name?

NICK: Goya.

EVA: Sounds like you've tasted something awful, goya. I had a raw oyster once, that was like—goya—

NICK: Yeah, I think oysters may be an acquired taste.

EVA: Acquiring a taste would require me to fall for that again.

NICK: Nice.

EVA: Do you like them?

NICK: Not really, no.

EVA: So. This Goya guy—

NICK: Francisco Goya. Spanish.

EVA: He painted war?

NICK: He did.

EVA: And are his paintings beautiful?

NICK: A terrible beauty.

EVA: Really?

NICK: he had a taste for it, I think.

EVA: Was he a pervert or something?

NICK: Not a pervert. Perverted, maybe, by the things he saw. He didn't start by painting the horrors of war. He was a lovely painter, a master. He painted enchanting portraits of women and children. But he lived through the Napoleonic Wars, and that kind of twisted him. From then on, he only painted terrible dark paintings. But they are still the work of a master. Extraordinarily powerful, amazing use of colour. He was painting his heart out, mourning the terrible things that happened to his country.

EVA: A fella took me to the opera once, on a date. I thought I would hate it. I went because I thought I liked the guy. You'd think I wouldn't have a clue about what was going on, because it's all sung in another language, but—I sure would like to see another.

NICK: No second date?

EVA: Turned out I liked opera, and not the guy.

Loved the opera . . . when we got to the end of the story, the woman, she's been betrayed, she's been abandoned, she is wrecked. And she sings. It's like her heart comes out of her in shattered little pieces. All her grief comes out of her in the most beautiful way. I cried and cried.

NICK: Opera is good at that. Tragedy made beautiful with music and voice.

EVA: maybe that's what you can do. Make tragedy beautiful with paint and canvas.

NICK looks at her.

what

NICK: A brain *and* a pretty face.

EVA: I should go and get ready to do my show. You gonna come?

NICK: I wouldn't miss it.

EVA: It ain't art.

NICK: A girl's gotta make a living.

EVA exits, singing.

EVA: "I'll be seeing you
In all the old familiar places
That this heart of mine embraces
All day through . . . "*

* "I'll Be Seeing You," Irving Kahal and Sammy Fain, 1938.

Newman 3

NICK is painting. NEWMAN approaches him from behind. He is wearing a uniform with a kilt. His face is white, the sockets of his eyes grey. He watches over NICK's shoulder.*

NEWMAN: I don't really look like that. Can't you paint what I really look like?

NICK: No no no no no

NEWMAN: These guys look like ghouls—their eyes are empty—like sharks' eyes—this guy looks like his eyes have been pecked away by birds. Do I look like that to you?

NICK: Newman. You can't be here.

NEWMAN: oh I get it—the soldiers who are helping these people, they are the walking dead. They've lost their humanity from their experiences in the war and that's why they have dead eyes. Hey, I'm good at this.

NEWMAN steps around from behind NICK and NICK sees him for the first time.

NICK: Jesus.

---

* See *The Conquerors*, formerly called *The Victims*, Eric Kennington, 1920.

NEWMAN: No, Newman.

NICK: What the hell are you wearing?

NEWMAN: My uniform.

NICK: That's not your uniform.

NEWMAN: It's not?

NICK: I don't even think that uniform is worn anymore. Not this war.

NEWMAN: Nick. You know, maybe you should talk to someone.

NICK laughs.

NICK: it's amazing that I am getting advice from you and I am actually considering it, as if that's perfectly normal.

NEWMAN: There is nothing normal about this, but . . . we can take a lot, Nick. It is amazing how much the human mind can take, see men blown up, slip on guts, a boot with a foot still in it, and we just keep going. Well, most of us.

NICK: Most of us.

NEWMAN: Yes. You gotta keep taking it or you *will* lose it. You'll be one of those blubberers in the booby hatch. And you're not just gone for the war, buddy. You are gone for good. You don't come back from where they've gone.

NICK starts to cry.

Aw, no, aw come on now, Nick, this is not good. Think of Fran. Be strong for Fran. D'you have a picture of her?

NICK: A picture?

NEWMAN: Yeah. A photo. You carry something with you?

NICK: Yes.

NEWMAN: Well, let's see it then.

NICK pulls a letter out of his left breast pocket. He slips a photo out of the letter. NEWMAN looks over his shoulder at it.

Whoa. She's a beauty, Nick, you lucky dog. Where's that taken?

NICK: Home. Nova Scotia. Our backyard.

NEWMAN: And that's where she is now, Nova Scotia?

NICK nods.

Nova Scotia. A good place for her to be. A good place for you to go back to, when this is all over. I'd like to come and visit some day. I'd never seen the sea before this, you know. I'd like to see it in peacetime though.

NICK: I've never been to Saskatchewan.

NEWMAN: Oh, you should. It's like a sea, too. That's what I thought when I finally saw it, it's just like Saskatchewan, only wet. Fields as far as the eye can see, waves of grain, green or gold or yellow, swaying and rocking in the wind. The sun heading for the horizon, that perfect light. And the smell of good, rich earth, and things growing. You should come and paint that. Well, except for the smell, you can't paint that.

NICK: That's what I'd like to paint.

NEWMAN: Attaboy! Paint the smell! Paint it so that anyone standing there in Halifax can inhale and smell the fields of Saskatchewan. Yes!

NICK picks up his sketchbook.

Hey, you gonna do me?

NICK: Just a quick sketch.

NEWMAN: You want me to sit? Stand? How about this? Something heroic? Something tragic.

NICK: Just sit. Still.

As NICK sketches him:

NEWMAN: Dead horses, dead women, dead cows—it's bound to get to a guy after a while. Do some more portraits of the living. Paint some landscapes. At least the landscape is living.

NICK: Like when I first met up with you over here.

NEWMAN: What?

NICK: I was painting a copse, just practising.

NEWMAN: See? always with the dead—

NICK: a copse, Newman, a stand of trees

NEWMAN: oh

NICK ignores him.

NICK: They didn't send me over here to paint pastoral Europe. They sent me here to paint dead horses, dead women, dead cows.

He sketches a bit more.

NEWMAN: Don't need any more pretty pictures of Europe anyway. Place is lousy with them.

NICK: Rich with them. When I first came over, every chance I got, I went to the local museum, the art galleries. Everywhere, work by masters, by forgotten artists, in the churches, in the town halls. After a while it made me kind of homesick. Not for what I saw there, but for what I didn't.

NEWMAN: I don't follow

NICK: Made me wonder what the folks at home would feel if they could walk into a gallery or a church and see art that—connected them. To where they live. Where we live.

NEWMAN: You should paint Canada.

NICK: I haven't been very many places in Canada.

NEWMAN: But you've been *some* places.

NICK: Hold still. I could paint Nova Scotia. I could paint the sea.

NEWMAN: Paint the Rocky Mountains.

NICK: I've never been to the Rocky Mountains.

NEWMAN: you could go, though.

NICK: I saw a painting once, by a woman, of the trees out west. All dark greens and imposing.

NEWMAN: I bet it's different from where you live.

NICK: I bet it is.

NEWMAN: Now, don't go giving me those empty eyes.

NICK: I won't.

NEWMAN: 'Cause if I'm going to be immortalized, then I want to be looking good. All my bits intact, my eyes wide open with the light in 'em.

NICK: You got it.

NEWMAN: Nick—Nickie—

NEWMAN tenses, arches.

NICK: Newman, you have to sit still, or else—Newman?

NEWMAN starts to slide off the rock.

Photographer

EVA: *(sings)* "I don't want to set the world on fire
I just want to start a flame in your heart
In my heart I have but one desire
And that one is you, no other will do"*

NICK has a plate of food, which he is sort of pushing around.

DENNIS: Mind if I sit here?

NICK shakes his head. DENNIS sits.

It's not exactly Chateaubriand, is it?

NICK: I'm not even sure it's meat.

DENNIS: Still, it feeds the furnace. I'm grateful to be able to partake. When I parachuted into France with the 13th Parachute Battalion—it was days before we had anything other than rat packs—couldn't light a fire, not even to make a cup of tea—

NICK: You travel with the British forces, then?

DENNIS: The Brits, the Yanks, the Canucks occasionally. Wherever the action is. I'm not enlisted, so I go where I please.

---

* "I Don't Want to Set the World on Fire," Eddie Seiler, Sol Marcus, Bennie Benjamin, and Eddie Durham, 1938.

NICK nods.

My name's Dennis. Photographer.

NICK: Yeah, so Newman was saying.

DENNIS: Ah, my reputation precedes me.

NICK: Well, I only—

DENNIS: You know, I met another one of your type—

NICK: My type?

DENNIS: A painter

NICK: Ah

DENNIS: Not a bad fellow. Convivial. We became chummy. And one day he invited me to his studio to see what he was working on. It was a painting of a photograph, with a portrait of a bunch of the brass in front, almost like caught by the lens.

NICK: I'm not sure I understand.

DENNIS: It was huge, took up the whole wall. He had painted an aerial photograph of some city. In front of the huge aerial photograph stood a bunch of officers. Some of them were posed *(poses)*, but others were going about their business, looking at the aerial, checking clipboards, et cetera. Someone had stuck a sheet of paper to the wall aerial.

NICK: It sounds clever.

DENNIS: It was a painting of a *photograph*. Two photos, actually. The artist was painting the officers from a photograph as well.

NICK: Lots of artists paint from photographs. It's sometimes hard—

DENNIS: Look, no offence intended, but—painting is passé.

NICK: Passé?

DENNIS: Obsolete.

NICK: How can it be obsolete? Most Canadians have never even seen a painting

DENNIS: Exactly! But most Canadians *have* seen a photograph. Everything they know about this war comes from photographs. We will know more about this war than any other because of photography.

NICK: Don't you think there's room for us both?

DENNIS laughs.

DENNIS: I suppose. Just as there's room for horsemen charging down on tanks screaming like banshees, but what's the point? They don't stand a chance. Look, my dear boy—

NICK: Nick.

DENNIS: Nick—things are moving fast. Everything is accelerated. The weaponry this war is more sophisticated than the last war, the communications equipment, the military strategy. Pretty soon we won't even have to see the people we are killing. Hand-to-hand combat will be just a story we tell our grandchildren.

NICK: I don't know if that's a good thing.

DENNIS: It is if it shortens the length of the combat.

NICK: It might extend it if we can't see who we're killing. That we are in fact killing.

DENNIS: War is evolving, and so is the way we document war. I'm a photographer, but I can already feel the filmmakers breathing down my neck. They're too unwieldy right now, I can go places no moviemaker can go, but it's only a matter of time before the technology catches up, and then still photography will be obsolete. The Germans are madly recording things—we know this—filming things. Imagine the documentation that will exist after this war.

NICK: I met a woman, a refugee, who called what the Germans are doing pornography.

DENNIS: Oh grow up.

NICK: That's a mature response.

DENNIS: I suppose she was a Jew.

NICK: I don't know.

DENNIS: Anyway, childish moral judgments aside, by the next war they will be able to do these things with no lapse in time—the whole world will be able to see war as it happens.

NICK: The next war.

DENNIS: Oh come on, Nick. Surely you don't believe that this war will end all wars. That was the moniker of the last one.

NICK: But that's what we're supposed to be doing, you and me and your friend with the aerial photo. Taking these images back home, forcing people to face them—

DENNIS: I don't force anyone to face anything. People are hungry for photographs. They buy newspapers, *Life* magazine, *Look* magazine, *Time* . . . They want the news while it's fresh.

NICK: Of course they do.

DENNIS: By the time you produce one . . . painting . . . the public's attention will be elsewhere, on the next war, or the next movie star, or whatever.

NICK: you have a very dim view of the public

DENNIS: They want instant gratification. They're voracious consumers of news, and that's what I give them. Instant storytelling. This is what is happening here now. What story are you going to tell them?

NICK: I am going to tell them this is what war feels like.

DENNIS: who cares what war feels like?

NICK: we have to care. We have to understand the cost.

DENNIS: Dear boy—

NICK: Nick.

DENNIS: Nick. The public consumes these things as entertainments. Even if some housewife from Toledo is moved by something you or I show her, she goes, "Oh, how horrible," and then she goes back to peeling potatoes for dinner for her son who is just dying to sign up to go somewhere with a gun.

NICK: no, that's just it. We have to make the connections for them. This soldier in this painting, this is your son.

DENNIS: It's not my job to interpret.

NICK: Oh come on now. Your camera isn't going off by itself, you are attached to it.

DENNIS: So?

NICK: your photographs are completely objective

DENNIS: The subjectivity is in the viewer, not the photographer.

NICK: And you don't influence the viewer in any way

DENNIS: I don't try—

NICK: that's incredibly naive.

DENNIS: I'm naive? You're the one plodding around Europe with paints and brushes.

NICK: At least I am aware that I interpret what I see.

DENNIS: A painting of a photo. Why don't you pick up a camera?

NICK: I *am* a camera.

Magda 2

MAGDA enters. NICK is painting furiously, attacking the paper with his brushes, with charcoal, with paint. MAGDA watches him for a moment.

MAGDA: What's this? A new style?

NICK: It's called impotence.

MAGDA: Waste of paint.

NICK: Ever since I landed.

MAGDA: Don't be a baby.

NICK shrugs.

NICK: I have some bread, Magda

NICK digs in his pack.

and more chocolate. Here.

MAGDA takes the bread, begins to eat it.

MAGDA: In my previous life this would not be bread I would eat.

NICK: It's not very good, is it?

MAGDA: It's terrible.

NICK: I know.

MAGDA: Eating makes me sad these days. When I eat . . . I remember the life I lived before this one. A civilized life. It seems like a dream. It's easier if I think of it as a dream. I lived in a large European city, in a modern flat. In the mornings I arose from my bed, I put my hair up with a couple of ivory combs, and I went to the bakery with my basket on my arm. I met my neighbours on the street, and we exchanged pleasantries, "Good morning, Mrs. Adler. Good morning, Mrs. Strauss." In the bakery I chose whatever warm bread I wanted for the day, sometimes a sweet pastry for breakfast, full of nuts and spices and sugar. If the bread was not warm, I did not choose it. I filled my basket with the bread and the newspaper, and I went home and made coffee. I heated milk and added sugar, two full teaspoons, every cup. I sat down at my beautiful wooden table with my sweet café latte and my sweet buns and I read all about the coming war, and I *(clucks her tongue)* and I shook my head.

NICK: I'm sorry.

MAGDA: I am one of the lucky ones. This is luck.

NICK: Me too. I only pick up a gun to pretend I'm a soldier. I've never had to shoot anyone. All I have to do is record what I see.

MAGDA: My days are full of the work of survival. Wake up in a barn or a house or wood and be grateful I am not yet discovered. Spend the day searching for something to eat, hide from people who would turn me in, look for the next safe place to lie for the night. I am reduced to an animal. But my luck is better than yours maybe. You are given food and shelter and time so that you can remain open to what you see.

NICK: Well, I have seen just about all I want to see.

MAGDA: there's more.

Artist

NICK is painting. He is so still that at first MATTHAEUS does not see him as he walks on. He is carrying a large rucksack. They see each other at the same moment. NICK looks to his gun and sees it is not within reach. MATTHAEUS raises his hands in surrender. NICK shows him it is a brush he holds.

MATTHAEUS: You are a painter.

NICK: Yes.

MATTHAEUS: I am also.

NICK: Is that so?

MATTHAEUS: It is so.

NICK: You're not a soldier then.

MATTHAEUS laughs.

MATTHAEUS: No. Not a soldier.

NICK: You look like you should be a soldier.

MATTHAEUS: I do look like? Well, I am not. Are you? You wear the uniform, but you carry a brush.

NICK reaches for his gun.

NICK: I have a gun.

MATTHAEUS: I see. What kind of soldier carries brushes?

NICK: It's my job. To paint the war.

MATTHAEUS: I did not think the Americans were that smart, to send painters to war.

NICK: Canadian.

MATTHAEUS: Ah. Canadian. I am sorry. My ear is not—

NICK: What are you doing here?

MATTHAEUS: I am—I am—

NICK: Yes?

MATTHAEUS: I am escaping.

NICK: Deserting, you mean?

MATTHAEUS laughs again.

Why are you laughing?

MATTHAEUS: It is—I do not know the word in English—*die Ironie*—that I have come so far to be captured by a . . . painter.

NICK: Well, painter or not, I am still a soldier, and if you are a soldier—deserting or not—I still have to take you captive.

MATTHAEUS: I am not a soldier. I was once a soldier. I have the Iron Cross.

NICK: With you?

MATTHAEUS: No. Not with me. I left it.

MATTHAEUS lowers his rucksack and starts to open it. NICK lunges for his gun and points it at MATTHAEUS. MATTHAEUS raises his hands again and gingerly nudges the rucksack toward NICK.

Please. You look.

A pause. Then NICK warily peers into the rucksack, gun still on MATTHAEUS.

NICK: It's—a painting?

MATTHAEUS: A painting, yes. Two pieces of one painting, to speak truly.

NICK steps back.

NICK: All right, take it out.

MATTHAEUS gingerly reaches into the rucksack, takes out a piece of plywood. He holds it up to NICK to show him what it is. NICK lowers his gun.

Oh my god.

MATTHAEUS: Yes.

NICK: It looks like—a crucifixion.

MATTHAEUS: Yes. But it is not our God being crucified, it is—

NICK: A soldier.

MATTHAEUS: Yes.

NICK: But where is the rest of it?

MATTHAEUS: I have another piece. I may get it?

NICK nods, still looking at the first piece. MATTHAEUS extracts the second piece.

NICK: But—where—where's the rest of it?

MATTHAEUS: The other twenty-three pieces are—

MATTHAEUS makes a scattering motion.

—verstreúen—

NICK: Scattered?

MATTHAEUS: Scattered, yes.

NICK: But who would do this to a piece of art?

MATTHAEUS: I did it.

NICK: You did.

MATTHAEUS: Yes. Well, I was helped by the owner of the—

MATTHAEUS makes a motion.

—saege—

NICK: Saw?

MATTHAEUS: Saw factory.

NICK: Sawmill.

MATTHAEUS: Ah yes. Sawmill.

NICK: . . .

MATTHAEUS: This hand belongs to the soldier who is crucified. He is wearing a mask against the gas.

NICK: A gas mask.

MATTHAEUS: Yes. There are other soldiers around the foot of the cross.

MATTHAEUS props up the two pieces of painting.

On this—

He motions to the empty space to the right of the pieces.

NICK: There's more? Section? Panel?

MATTHAEUS: Yes, panel. On this panel there are kneeling figures, old and young, a child, a dog. There is a woman, but her face is turned away from the cross. At the bottom of the panel, flowers.

NICK: There is another panel here?

NICK motions to the other side.

It's a triptych?

MATTHAEUS: A triptych. Yes. And on this panel more soldiers, *der bischof*, soldiers with guns and—

MATTHAEUS motions.

—*das seitengewehr*

NICK: Bayonet.

MATTHAEUS: Just so. And in this corner, a baby a flag holding. And more flowers.

NICK: you . . . cut it up?

MATTHAEUS: they were coming for me, I imagine they would not leave my work

NICK: They were coming for you?

MATTHAEUS: Yes. I am fortunate to still have friends

MATTHAEUS motions.

NICK: in high places?

MATTHAEUS: Yes, in high places. Who tell me that I will be arrested. So I take my painting that makes them so angry and we cut it up. I give pieces to friends, friends who are safe, friends who will be able to escape things out of Germany. The people who own the sawmill, they keep one piece. I take these pieces with me. In case I escape. I still have something of my work, of my life.

NICK: But if you have the Iron Cross, then you are a war hero.

MATTHAEUS: The first war. Yes.

NICK: And you're obviously an important artist.

MATTHAEUS: You are kind.

NICK: So why would they arrest you?

MATTHAEUS: Because I would not paint his portrait.

It was a test, of course. No one cares who paints the *führer*'s portrait. There are better painters of portraits than me. But I refused. And they knew.

NICK: But why didn't you just paint it?

MATTHAEUS: I can only paint what I see. Imagine if I painted the inside of this man, put it on the outside, on the canvas for the world to see.

NICK: You couldn't have just painted a straight portrait?

MATTHAEUS: Paint a lie?

NICK: You tell the truth, just tell it slant.

MATTHAEUS: Is this what you do?

MATTHAEUS holds out his hand for NICK's sketchbook. NICK holds it closer to himself.

NICK: I don't know what I do. My friend Newman says I should go home and paint the sea and the fields of grain and the mountains, but I don't know if I will be able to paint . . . peace.

MATTHAEUS comes to NICK, peels the book from him. He slowly flips through the pages.

Sometimes I want to live just so I can paint these things.

MATTHAEUS: and other times?

NICK: sometimes I think it would be easier to die here than carry these images around for the rest of my life.

MATTHAEUS: This man—this young man—he appears here—and here—and here—he is your friend?

NICK: He is someone I know. Yes.

MATTHAEUS: He is alive?

Now NICK *laughs.*

NICK: Oh no, I think he is quite dead. He has certainly died enough.

MATTHAEUS: But here he lives again.

NICK *grabs the book back.*

NICK: Here he dies again. And again. And again. I cannot paint him enough deaths to give him peace.

MATTHAEUS: Peace.

NICK: I see him die every day.

MATTHAEUS: you tell the truth about your friend in each of these sketches. All different, slant, as you say. But you tell the truth about you too. You cannot help it. You see why I could not paint the portrait?

NICK *nods.* MATTHAEUS *goes back to where the two pieces of painting are propped up. He chooses one, returns to* NICK, *hands it to him.*

Take this painting with you.

NICK: I can't.

MATTHAEUS: With your other work, your other paintings. At least one will be saved if I do not get out.

NICK: No one who looks at it will believe it's mine.

MATTHAEUS: No one will look at it now. Slip it into your *stápel* of canvases. Who looks at what a painter makes? In a few years they shake their heads that this piece did not tell on itself, that they did not see it being smuggled out of Germany.

NICK: Why not give me both pieces?

MATTHAEUS: Because at least this one

MATTHAEUS putting the remaining piece back into his rucksack.

will be saved if you don't make it out.

NICK: And what if I don't let you go?

MATTHAEUS: Then I will give you both.

NICK: All right. Go.

MATTHAEUS begins to leave.

Wait.

MATTHAEUS stops.

What's it called? This cut-up painting of yours.

MATTHAEUS: It is called *Thou Shalt Not Kill.*

Newman 4

EVA: *(sings)* "I'll be seeing you
In all the old familiar places
That this heart of mine embraces
All day through"*

NICK is frantically flipping through canvases, ripping out pages from his sketchbook, matching them up. Sometimes he matches two or three pages to a canvas, but the exercise seems only to be frustrating him, not satisfying.

NEWMAN appears. He is in another uniform, another war, another era, possibly from the future, this century. Maybe the blue beret?

NEWMAN: Wow, Nickie, easy. You're gonna hurt something.

NICK: hello, Newman

NEWMAN imitates him.

NEWMAN: "Hello, Newman." I thought you'd be glad to see me.

NICK: *now* what are you wearing?

NEWMAN: my uniform

---

* "I'll Be Seeing You," Sammy Fain and Irving Kahal, 1938.

NICK: that's not your uniform.

NEWMAN: it isn't?

NICK: I've never seen anything like that

NEWMAN looks at the painting.

NEWMAN: looking good, Nickie

NICK: It needs to be oils.

NEWMAN: Oils?

NICK: watercolours are too . . . transparent. Light goes through the colour and bounces back off the white paper at the viewer.

NEWMAN: Oh yeah, I can see that.

NICK: It's all wrong for this kind of . . . subject matter.

NEWMAN: there's rules?

NICK: not really rules. More of a feeling. It should be oils so that the light can't go through, so that it just stops there, on the surface, on the image.

NEWMAN: Hah. I never even knew there was a difference.

NICK: watercolours are for hopeful things, beautiful things—

NEWMAN: Guess you can't work with oils out here.

NICK: Too messy, complicated. The dirt. Drying time. You have to layer them.

NEWMAN: when you get home, you'll do this again in oils, right? Paint it better?

NICK: Paint it better.

NEWMAN: you know, you keep repeating what I say

NICK: you're right, Newman, I want to paint the whole damn thing better. I keep filling these books with sketches

all these images trapped inside me. And I don't know how I feel about these things, how can I even know what I feel until I get them outside of me

"don't worry about it," the brass says, "you'll have time later to paint, just keep grabbing the images, put them together after"

after?

all of this

He indicates the sketches:

in my mind until I get home.

So I steal time to vomit some of this out—the dead soldier half buried in mud, the burned airman, the boot with the foot in it—

I need to know how these things go together . . . what am I saying? Will anyone care?

Newman?

Newman?

But NEWMAN is gone.

Belsen

DENNIS: what are you doing here, Nick? Thought this was a British party—

NICK: British Canadian. I was dispatched to record the liberation of this camp

DENNIS: Well, I hope you are not expecting joyful faces or tears of gratitude . . . I heard the photographer who was at the "liberation" of Buchenwald couldn't even speak—of course she's a woman—

NICK: I heard about Buchenwald. I wouldn't be here if I wasn't ordered.

DENNIS: are you kidding? This is news. The Nazis destroyed other camps on their way out—

NICK: Treblinka.

DENNIS: Sobibor. Another one—I forget the name—so it's good that we got to Belsen before they could raze it.

if you haven't got the stomach for it, Nick, just hang back. Let the professionals deal with it.

Tell you what. I'll take photos and give you a few, and you can paint from those. Like your friend there, with the aerial photo and the generals standing around, that you thought was so clever. You can turn my photos into art.

NICK: funny

DENNIS: did you bring rations?

NICK: no. why?

DENNIS: one thing we do know, these people are going to be hungry.

NICK feels in his pockets.

NICK: I have a bar of chocolate—

DENNIS: here we go—

DENNIS goes to lift his camera and stops.

oh my god

NICK looks, sees what DENNIS is seeing. The denizens of the concentration camp are indeed overjoyed to see the liberators but look like walking skeletons. DENNIS lifts the camera to his eye and shoots. Then he lowers the camera, turns away, and pukes. The prisoners begin to understand the way they must look and turn away from the fence. One woman walks toward the three men. She is impossibly skinny, in rags.

NICK: Magda? Magda?

DENNIS lifts his camera and starts to shoot again.

MAGDA stops, turns, and walks away. She lies down, curling a bit, fetal-like. She becomes one of the dead. NICK follows her, sets down his pack, takes out his sketchbook.

Completion

NICK is packing up his work. NEWMAN enters.

NEWMAN: What's the first thing you're gonna do when you get home, Nickie?

NICK: The first thing? I guess I'll hug Fran, she'll be there to meet me. I'll hug her and kiss her and hold her until she wiggles. Then I'll hold her away from me like this

NICK grabs NEWMAN and holds him at arm's length and looks at him.

and look at her, and then I'll hug her again.

He pulls NEWMAN close for a hug. They embrace for a moment, then pull apart.

NEWMAN: And then?

NICK: Then we'll go somewhere for something to eat. And I'll sit across from her and just look at her some more. Do you think we'll ever be able to talk again? I'm not the same person who went away.

NEWMAN: None of us are, Nick.

NEWMAN flips through the canvases. We see MATTHAEUS's piece, perhaps.

Looks like the war really made an artist outta you, Nick

NICK: Got a lot of work to do yet. The military's setting us up with studio space in Canada.

> *NEWMAN is flipping through NICK's work. He finds his face everywhere.*

NEWMAN: Jesus, Nick. I'm flattered, I guess. But—don't you have any other friends?

NICK: Don't know how long we'll have, so I'll have to work fast, get these out of here

> *He holds up his sketchbook.*

and here

> *He taps his head.*

and onto canvas

NEWMAN: attaboy

NICK: Memento mori.

NEWMAN: What kind of mementos?

NICK: Let me tell you, Newman, once I finish these—whatever they turn out to be—I will never paint another dead body.

NEWMAN: So, paint live ones.

NICK: I will paint living bodies into the Canadian landscape, just like you told me to.

NEWMAN: I told you?

NICK: Paint Canada, you said.

You don't remember, Newman, but I do. Paint Nova Scotia, you said. Paint the sea. Paint the back step. Paint the smell in Saskatchewan.

NEWMAN: I told you to paint the smell in Saskatchewan? I musta been outta my head.

NICK: And in honour of you, my undying friend Newman, I am going to paint Canada.

EVA: *(sings)* "Ev'ry time we say goodbye
I die a little
Ev'ry time we say goodbye
I wonder why a little

Why the Gods above me
Who must be in the know
Think so little of me
They allow you to go"*

Time telescopes to 2005. The new Canadian Museum of War. HEATHER stands before a painting. She is making an address.

HEATHER: . . . it can be argued that the war made Canadian art and Canadian artists, who in turn made Canada. A. Y. Jackson, Arthur Lismer, and Frederick Varley were war artists during the First World War, Lawren Harris during the Second World War, all original members of the Group of Seven.

Alex Colville, who has been referred to as the "painter laureate" of Canada, was also a war artist during the Second World War, as was

* "Ev'ry Time We Say Goodbye," Cole Porter, 1944.

Charles Comfort, who went on to run the National Gallery. Dozens of other artists, lesser known, as well as enlisted men—soldiers who painted—contributed to a body of war art.

For a long time these works had no permanent home and so were warehoused in various spaces around the nation's capitol. In 1968 R.F. Wodehouse created a checklist of the war collection of World War One and World War Two, a massive undertaking that counted over 5,400 pieces.

The artists who came back painted work both horrific and heroic, work that inspired, informed, and commented on the reality and the unreality of war. Moreover, art that had seemed unaffordable and elitist during the Depression became accessible and vital to the psyche of a young nation.

Works by these artists changed the course of Canadian art. Canadians were able to see what their role in the wars had been, and the cost of that role. Not only did the war artists transform Canada, they were in turn transformed by their experiences in wartime, making their painting of this country even richer—a land free from the destruction that Europe had suffered. They painted Canada with new eyes, and in turn gave us a new appreciation of this land.

Applause, which HEATHER *acknowledges, then begins to gather up her things: speaking notes, laptop, phone, glasses, water bottle, whatever.*

NICK, *old now, approaches her. Stands a bit awkwardly.*

Hello.

NICK *nods.*

Are you—

NICK: Thank you.

HEATHER: Oh well, thank you for coming.

Beat.

Are you . . . a veteran?

NICK: Yes.

HEATHER: well—

Beat.

Thank you for your service.

NICK nods.

NICK: I am also a painter.

HEATHER: A painter? You're one of the—?

NICK: I have two paintings in here.

HEATHER: Two?

NICK: That are displayed. And more still in the warehouse, I think.

NICK chuckles.

My broom closet.

HEATHER: Really?

NICK nods.

NICK: It's good that there are at least two out of the broom closet. I didn't think I'd ever see them again.

HEATHER: will you show them to me?

NICK: You know them already. You used them in your slide show.

HEATHER: I did? Are you—wow—I am so pleased to meet you, Mr.—

NICK: It's Nick. Just Nick. Please.

He chuckles.

Shaking his head.

Photographs of my paintings.

Beat.

Shall we go see the real thing?

NICK offers her his arm. She takes it and slowly they exit.

Acknowledgements

The Art of War was commissioned in 2015 by Persephone Theatre, where it received developmental support and workshop readings under the dramaturgy of DD Kugler. Further development was made possible through the Canada Council for the Arts, SK Arts, the University of Saskatchewan, On the Boards Staging Company, and the Saskatchewan Festival of Words. Thanks to all the artists who participated in its development, including Kate Herriot, Bruce McKay, Nathan Howe, Joshua Beaudry, Lauren Allen, Jonathan Geenan, Marc Richard, Charlotte Moore, Ralph Small, and David Copelin. My apologies to anyone I have forgotten.

Yvette Nolan (Algonquin) is a playwright, director, and dramaturg who works across Turtle Island. Her works include the plays *Annie Mae's Movement*, *The Unplugging*, *The Diviners* (with Vern Thiessen), *Reasonable Doubt* (with Joel Bernbaum and Lancelot Knight), the dance-opera *Bearing*, the libretto *Shawnadithit*, and the short film *A Common Experience* (with Shane Belcourt). From 2003 to 2011 she served as Artistic Director of Native Earth Performing Arts. Her book *Medicine Shows*, about Indigenous performance in Canada, was published by Playwrights Canada Press in 2015, and *Performing Indigeneity* (co-edited with Ric Knowles) in 2016.